YOUR FREE CURRICULUM
$20 VALUE

Jeub's Guide to Speech & Debate comes with a simple, easy-to-understand group of lessons that is perfect for teachers, coaches, administrators and students. Visit the following link for complete information.

www.trainingminds.org/jeub-curriculum
Use code: XJEUB13

Chris Jeub's legacy includes several national champions and hundreds of young leaders who have honed their skills through forensics. For his efforts, Jeub is rightly regarded as a leader in speech and debate and has earned this platform.

—*Cody Herche*
Author, Keys to Cross-Examination

When I started competing, I was hooked! The culture was by far the healthiest I had ever seen, and I didn't have to be a genius to realize what a positive impact it was having on me. Mr. Jeub's book accurately and convincingly describes the community and environment that made this sport such a hit for me and my family.

—*John-Micah Braswell*
Stoa Competitor, Colorado

Chris Jeub's leadership is apparent. His materials are vital components to the development of successfully competitive, tournament-ready speech and debate students. Whether the students are novices or advanced, Chris's speech and debate resources cover everything a coach needs and everything students need. His training information is well organized, comprehensive, and unmatched.

—*Carmen Dampf*
COMMAND AZ Speech & Debate Club

Speech & debate is not just an extra-curricular activity, it's a complete life changer. I wish Jeub's Guide to Speech & Debate *had been out when I got started. If you're considering getting involved, or you're not sure how leagues or clubs or tournaments work, or you have any other question, you can't afford* not *to have this book. Get one for yourself, and a few more for your friends.*

—*Travis Herche*
Professional Speech & Debate Coach

In a world where communication is essential for success in life and so many students have difficulty with even the simplest forms of expression, Chris Jeub provides the kind of foundational guidelines that lead to excellence. Jeub's Guide to Speech and Debate *is more than a guide to help students win contests. It will enable students to excel at life.*

—*Ken Davis*
SCORRE Conferences
Author and Story Teller, Fully Alive

Jeub's Guide to
Speech & Debate

Mastering the Competitive Culture of the Forensic Sport

Chris Jeub

MONUMENT PUBLISHING
think, speak, persuade.

Jeub's Guide to Speech & Debate

5th Edition

Published by
Monument Publishing
P.O. Box 3527
Monument, CO 80132

ISBN: 978-1-936147-49-6

Manufactured in the United States of America

First Printing, January 2013

www.monumentpublishing.com

Contents

Foreword by Andrew Pudewa 5

Introduction 9

    About Me, Chris Jeub 10
    The Big Idea 11

1. Educational Options 15

    Three Educational Choices 18
        Home Education 18
        Public Education 19
        Private Education 19
    Time Commitment 20
    Organizations 22
        NCFCA 22
        Stoa 24
        NFL 27
        Other Organizations 28
    Resources to Help 29
        Your School's Curriculum 29

2. Speech 33

    Platform Speaking 34
        Original Oratory 34
        Expository 35
        Persuasive 37
    Literary Interpretation 38
        Humorous 40
        Dramatic 40
        Duo 40
    Other Speeches 41
        Prose, Poetry or Storytelling 41
        Original Interpretation 41
        Open Interpretation 42
        Wildcards 42
    Resources 42
        Bronze Book 43
        Keys to Interp 44
        Curriculum 44

3. Limited Preparation 47

    Impromptu 48

Extemporaneous 49
Apologetics 51
Resources.. 52
Gold Book 52
Keys to Extemp 53
Silver Book 53
Curriculum.. 54

4. *Debate*... **57**

Team-Policy 58
Team.. 58
Policy 61
"Blue" = Team-Policy Debate 62
Lincoln-Douglas 63
One-on-One Format 63
Values.. 64
"Red" = Lincoln-Douglas Debate 65
Public Forum.. 66
Parliamentary 68
Resources.. 69
Sourcebooks 69
Flowsheets 70
Curriculum.. 71

5. *Tournaments*... **73**

Calendar 73
Script Submission 74
Ethical Evidence 74
Read the Rules 75
Adjudication.. 75
Registration Deadlines 76
Judging Requirements 77
Family 77

6. *The C's to Success*... **81**

Camp.. 82
Coaching... 83
Curriculum.. 84
Sourcebooks & Textbooks 85
Keeping Score 86
Commitment 87

7. *Conclusion*... **91**

Acknowledgements *93*
Connect with Chris Jeub........................... *94*

FOREWORD BY ANDREW PUDEWA

Founder of the Institute for Excellence in Writing

We have graduated five of our seven children with two at home, ages 12 and 15, the perfect ages for speech and debate. My wife and I seek to finish our parenting race in the coming years, but we still face our challenges and doubts like any educator does, no matter how seasoned. As I pen this foreword for my friend Chris Jeub, it is the beginning of the competitive season for us, and I'm feeling my youthful self again.

I'd like to discuss the value of a formal public speaking program, and the truly remarkable culture of competitive forensics. Chris is in the middle of this essential, foundational discipline, and I hope my story will help encourage you to take the precepts in *Jeub's Guide to Speech & Debate* seriously.

Eight years ago, living in California, my Daughter #3 was 16 and coming into her home stretch. As she had become so proficient at arguing during her childhood, I thought she might do well in a formal setting, where argumentation was more structured and polite. Having met many debaters in my travels, I was always impressed with their poise and confident articulation and really felt it necessary to provide that opportunity for my daughter in the short time remaining. Unfortunately, the closest debate club was 90 miles away, which was just not practical for us at that time. However, I was unwilling to give up the idea entirely, and so with another family who was equally enthusiastic about the idea of debate for their two eldest, we started a club in our local area.

Of course, we had almost no clue what we were doing. We ordered up some books from Chris Jeub's website, got our little group of teenagers together, and started from the very beginning, learning the basics of debate format, collecting evidence, and building cases. The learning curve was steep. Using

Chris' resources and direction, we were ready enough to venture out to our first tournament in San Diego.

If you have never been to a speech and debate tournament before, I will tell you point-blank you are missing one of the greatest, most inspiring, truly awesome things happening on the planet. Imagine a hundred or more students professionally dressed, profoundly excited about standing in front of peers and judges, arguing for changes in medical malpractice law in an articulate and knowledgeable way, while practicing in between debate rounds persuasive or dramatic speeches for competition. Now, I must confess I am somewhat of a pessimist by nature and often find the world situation somewhat bleak, but going to that first tournament actually gave me hope for our world in a way I had never before experienced. I saw and heard these young men and women preparing themselves with the writing, speaking, teamwork, and leadership skills so desperately needed in our world today— they were in many ways demonstrating the best of the educational world as I knew it. I was profoundly inspired.

Of course, our two teams got slaughtered. They maybe won a single round, but oddly they weren't discouraged. If anything, they were more enthusiastic than ever to get back to work, gather and organize evidence, refine their cases, study vocabulary specific to the resolution, and practice delivery skills. We went to a few more tournaments that year, and although none had much of a win-loss record to show, all of them enjoyed the challenge and acknowledged the value of the effort they put into it. We were hooked.

The next year we got serious, starting in August with a "Speech Boot Camp," a two-week public speaking intensive, designed to help new students pass their initial resistance to public speaking and get used to writing, delivering, and critiquing several types of speeches. Our little camp was such a help that we created a DVD package we titled with the same name that we sell on our website to this day (*www.IEW.com/SBC-D*). Although three of our four original students graduated and went off to college, we talked it up and recruited enough new students to double our size; "The Liber" (our club name) had eight debaters, including my Daughter #4. It was a much better year, as we had a degree of experience under our belt and knew what to expect. By the following year, our club had doubled in size again; several of the second-year debaters planned to give platform or interpretive speeches; and we were encouraged to see tremendous growth in confidence and skills in all of the students, especially those who had been so shy and anxious in the beginning.

While it's inspiring and satisfying to see so many young people develop their communication skills through speech and debate, what's even more exciting for me is to see how the community so actively nurtures character development. With a wide age range of debaters (12 to 18), it is not at all uncommon to see a little 12-year-old girl cross-examining a six-foot 17-year-old boy, or vice versa. The supportive, gracious interaction between students of all ages and levels of experience demonstrates that the forensic world is truly one of social excellence.

Will debate take time? Yes, possibly a lot. Money? Yes, some, especially for travel. Will it be worth it? Absolutely. I am confident that if you were to ask a hundred graduates who did debate, "What were the most important or valuable things you did during your teen years?" they would overwhelmingly affirm that speech and debate was the most beneficial and formative, even—or perhaps especially—the ones who resisted the idea at first. My kids certainly would.

That's my story, and Chris Jeub's work has been a tremendous influence throughout our journey. If tournaments are the most exciting thing happening on the planet, Chris Jeub is in the middle of that excitement. We have sent several of our students to his Training Minds Camps over the years as well as loyally ordering the *Blue Book* every year it comes out. I have been consistently impressed with his tireless contributions to the speech and debate community. So impressed, in fact, that last year I hired his group to come to our home in Oklahoma and train my club for a mini-camp. My club feels more prepared than ever thanks to Chris Jeub and his team of Training Minds coaches.

As I stated at the onset, speech and debate makes me feel young again. We have our late-winter and spring schedule outlined with tournaments in our region. Our family and community look forward to this time of the year. I wish the same enthusiasm for you, your school, your home and your community.

Andrew Pudewa
www.excellenceinwriting.com

This is Andrew's club in Oklahoma. Training Minds Coach Vance Trefethen is giving a lecture on the upcoming debate topic.

INTRODUCTION

I took my first "real" teaching job in 1995. The job market in Minnesota was saturated with English teaching graduates – lots of ambition but little experience – so after two years of substitute teaching, I was getting desperate. My chances for a job were tight. I stretched my thin resume as far as I could stretch it in every interview I landed.

"Do you have any experience with debate or public speaking?" the principle asked in my umpteenth interview.

Sure! I have some experience with public speaking in college. Oh, and I joined Toastmasters in high school with an old friend. Of course I have experience with public speaking and (what did you say?) debate. Yeah, I like to argue with people.

Did I just say that?

Good thing the principle was as desperate as I was. "Great!" he replied. "You're going to coach debate."

And I was hired. I served in North Dakota and Minnesota for five years before relocating to Colorado, and those were tremendous years for my teaching career. I coached a team of debaters who – I must admit – taught me much more than I ever knew as a young teacher.

I didn't know the first thing about academic debate, and I don't think the principle cared too much that I didn't. What I ventured into, though, was the most remarkable academic activity that I had ever witnessed. I was mesmerized by the academic rigor these kids voluntarily put themselves through. And the outcome was second-to-none. These kids were absolutely brilliant. It didn't take more than a few tournaments before I realized,

Speech and debate is the best extracurricular activity students can take.

That's right. The *best*. I used to think the written word was the best – still very important, which is why I got an English Teaching degree in the first place. But forensics had it all! Critical thinking, public speaking, persuasion, rhetoric – the list of skills mastered by the debate student was long. Those five years of coaching in the upper Midwest taught me how to teach speech and debate activities, and the next decade launched me into publishing curriculum. I've literally made speech and debate my life. Why? Because...

I believe students who master speech and debate will master life and become the leaders our world needs.

Speech and debate changed my entire pedagogical outlook. And you know what? I believe it should change yours, too. Whether you're a student, teacher, parent or administrator, I want you to consider:

- Students, chase after the first-place prizes during your competitive years.

- Teachers, award your best students and volunteer at every tournament.

- Parents, be your kid's #1 fan *and* #1 coach *and* #1 teacher.

- Administrators, make sure forensics is valued just as high (if not, higher!) than other sports.

None of the above? You can participate as a judge at tournaments, volunteer to help at tournaments, and ask clubs to be a part of the training. Young people are eager to perform speeches and scrimmage for laypeople who believe in the youth. That could be you!

About Me, Chris Jeub

That should give you a peek into my fundamental passion surrounding speech and debate. But what is it about me that makes my opinion worth reading? Allow me to explain the fundamentals of my passion and the framework from which this book is built.

First, I'm a publisher and businessman. Sure, I started in education, but today I am self-employed running a nonprofit and a publishing company – most of which is geared toward academic speech and debate. I'm associated with several educational networks – public, private, charter and home education – building vast and deep relationships with leaders that go back several years. Because of this, I have good things to say about how *you* should be involved. This book guides you in how you can participate in speech and debate.

Second, I'm experienced. I suppose you could have guessed that. I've run the largest tournaments in the nation, served on the boards of leagues, and coached kids from across the nation – some who have turned into title winners. I'm long past those initial years of not knowing what to do, and I love to guide others through the wonderful world of speech and debate.

Third, I've got quite a track record. Training Minds, the organization I founded in 2001 to "train minds for action" hosts camps for academic speakers and debaters. Chances are good that the finalists at national tournaments are our alumni, which shows you that my guidance may bring your kids to the same success.

Finally, I've got passion. Bottom line: I believe in this stuff. Speech and debate are such important skills for young people. I cannot express enough how grateful I am that you've got this *guide*.

You'll be guided toward excellence in this wonderful community of speakers and debaters. This book is what you need. Let's begin with a big idea.

The Big Idea

At the time of writing this book, my club (named *Monumentum*) ran the first Stoa tournament of the year for Colorado. It took place in November – quite early in the year, a small tournament, only the most ambitious debaters attended. Before the day started, I sent all the competitors this letter:

> *Dear Competitor,*
>
> *I hope you're in for an AWESOME time at the tournament! My club sure is. We've been busy all week, very much looking forward to hosting the 80 debaters who will be joining together for debate tomorrow. Let me say a word about our theme, Dream Big.*
>
> *I believe so much in you. You're training your mind for action, for a big purpose. Think of all those great skills you are learning in debate. You'll learn and grow through every single round. The relationships you build with your fellow competitors will last a lifetime. It'll be exhausting, but you're being trained for big things.*
>
> *Do me this favor: aim beyond the trophy. We spend so much time focusing on competition that people think we're out for the trophy. We want you to win, sure, but that's just the first accomplishment. We want you to apply what you learn to the great purpose life has in store for you.*
>
> *Now THAT gets us excited! Don't settle for small, debater. Dream big.*

Do you catch that vision? Forgive me if I sound too sappy when I say "dream big." Perhaps it sounds sappy because dreams *without the tools to achieve those dreams* aren't very achievable. In fact, they seldom become reality.

But speakers and debaters are being equipped with the greatest communication tools dreamers need to make their dreams come true. I honestly believe that! And you're holding the book in your hands to sharpen those tools and make those dreams come true.

Are you ready to go through the wonderful world of speech and debate? This book is the best tool to get started. Enjoy the journey, and see you at some tournaments!

One of the most enjoyable pinnacles of my career
was running this national tournament
where 600 students gathered for competition in Colorado Springs.

Why so enjoyable?

Because I got to hand out over 200 awards,
shake each and every hand,
of the brightest students in the world.

CHAPTER 1

Educational Options

This chapter lays the framework for your forensics career. You likely fall into one of four audience groups:

1. Students
2. Teachers
3. Administrators
4. Coaches

Think about which one (or *ones*) you are. It'll make your experience through the wonderful world of speech and debate much richer, easier, and more successful. This book is designed for each of these audience groups.

The **student** is the child or teen who will work through the book to gain the knowledge necessary to build a speech and debate education. Typically, speech and debate is introduced as an option in school to 12- to 18-year-old secondary students. The student may be self-taught, part of a class or club, seeking supplementary knowledge on topics already known, or receiving personal coaching from someone who knows speech and debate very well. Wherever the student is in his or her academic career, *Jeub's Guide to Speech & Debate* is the text that will guide the student to excellence in speech and debate.

The **teacher** is driving the student (or classroom of students) to learn the ins and outs of speech and debate. They will use the material in this book as well as supplemental material for the specific categories of competition. The teacher understands the purpose of speech and debate, and likewise captures the vision for excellence. No doubt that *Jeub's Guide to Speech & Debate* will bring some new vision to the teacher's perspective. The best kind of teacher is one who doesn't care so much about individual talent, but sees potential in every student. If you have this perspective as a teacher, you will find *Jeub's Guide to Speech & Debate* perfect for your classroom. It will give you the fundamentals for a successful academic speech and debate atmosphere.

The **administrator** is the person who will make sure academic speech and debate remain a core curriculum in the district, school or home. This book is purposely thin, an easy read, and inexpensive enough to hand off to other administrators and teachers. Administrators have in their power the ability to place their school's focus on the most valuable educational activities. *Jeub's Guide to Speech & Debate* helps the administrator give top priority to speech and debate.

The **coach** is what I hope everyone reading this book eventually becomes. You see, there is much more about speech and debate than what is covered in *Jeub's Guide to Speech & Debate*. This is hardly the "complete" guide. Public speaking and the arts of persuasion are lifelong journeys, more "art" than "curriculum." Students who apply the teaching of this book may become champions, and teachers will undoubtedly be empowered to teach the students. I hope, then, that both become coaches.

This 5th edition is specifically tailored to train students, teachers, administrators and coaches the fundamentals – the "keys" – to establishing a successful speech and debate academic career. Naturally, there is crossover in all four audience groups. Consider:

- A **student** attends a class, "Introduction to Speech & Debate." She is shy and fearful, but her parents and guidance counselors recognize the need to gain a credit for her education in speech. *Jeub's Guide to Speech & Debate* is her text that starts her venture.

- A **student** has no speech and debate club in his area, but he desires to compete and make an attempt to get to a state, regional or national tournament. His parents know nothing about forensics, so he picks up *Jeub's Guide to Speech & Debate* to gain the knowledge necessary to make his ambitions a reality.

- A **teacher** has students who desire to build speaking skills, but she feels inadequate in teaching. She's a good teacher but lacks the understanding of how to effectively engage in speech and debate. She needs to become a student of the skills – learn as she goes – to be able to best teach her own students.

- An **administrator** wants to get a speech and debate program going in his school. He sees the value in such a program, but he's having difficulty convincing his board, his staff, and the families and students. *Jeub's Guide to Speech & Debate* is easily passed around to help everyone understand the great value of the program.

- A **coach** is a teacher at heart, but also a cheerleader. He prepares the way for a successful speech and debate competitor, and continues to refine the skills of the competitor as time goes by. A teacher may find himself coaching his students more than he thought he would … and that is good.

Most exciting is this: The student who grows to be the teacher and the coach. I have seen this in all the speech and debate communities throughout my decades of teaching and coaching. Those who have experienced success – some all the way to top awards at national events – can't help but return to the classroom or club and coach those new students coming down the pike.

Three Educational Choices

There are three choices in education today: home, private and public education. I've coached in all three. Each have their advantages and disadvantages, and each have their opportunities to "train minds for action" in speech and debate. Allow me to comment on each of these choices.

Home Education

Speech and debate is considered the "homeschool sport," and I've been thoroughly involved in training home educators in this sport since 1996. My wife and I are home educators who have participated in two homeschool forensics leagues. I tell you, this is an awesome community of people.

I was a public school teacher when my wife and I started home educating in the 1990's, back when the educational choice was a bit taboo. Most people questioned the validity of educating at home – in truth, we had many doubts ourselves – but that question is largely gone today. Home education has become a very common educational choice, and a most successful one. Studies show that homeschoolers, on the average, out-perform their public school counterparts by 30 to 37 percentile points in all subjects.[1]

But home education is as diverse as the families who choose its path. Today, it is difficult to tell who home schools and who doesn't. Many educational choices within public schools offer at-home supplements, and some at-home curricula are sanctioned and even encouraged by public schools. This past decade, laws favoring charter schools have become hugely popular, and these charter schools have adopted more flexible, parent-centered educational approaches that have, in turn, been academically successful.

---

[1] Michael Smith and Michael Farris, "Academic Statistics on Home Schooling," Legal Research Supplement, October 22, 2004. *http://www.hslda.org/docs/nche/ 000010/200410250.asp*

Home educators are typically academically focused, so it is no wonder that speech and debate has become "the homeschool sport." I'll explain later the various leagues available to families, but it is safe to say that most anywhere in the United States home educated students are able to participate in speech and debate.

Public Education

I made my debut into speech and debate in public education, as do most American students and educators. Students who aspire to compete in public schools will find a robust future in the National Forensic League (NFL), the league of some 80 years of history that includes all forms of education – home, private and public schools.

The way competition is set up within public schools is through extracurricular clubs. Sometimes these clubs are supplemented with classes in the district curriculum, but most of the time these are after-school clubs whose purpose is to train in speech and debate events and to travel to tournaments throughout their region or state.

Students are able to sign up for the club much like signing up for any extracurricular program. Sometimes, as is the case for many sports, home school students are able to join when they make special arrangements with the district, school, teacher or coach.

Private Education

Private schools have traditionally adopted the NFL rules and have competed in NFL tournaments. In fact, they are considered just as viable an option of competition as their public school counterparts. Homeschool students, too, are able to join private school teams just like they join public school teams.

It is worth mentioning here that educational choices vary from state to state, sometimes quite significantly. In California, for instance, home educators join co-ops that are – in the eyes of the state – considered private schools. Charter laws in many states have allowed all sorts of alternative schools that have a mixture of home, public and private educational values.

The scope of *Jeub's Guide to Speech & Debate* isn't to figure out which mold fits you best. You probably fall into one of these three options in one form or another (or a mixture of some sort). I hope to merely show you these three educational options to *guide* your way to a healthy speech and debate curriculum.

Time Commitment

Whatever form of educator you are or the kind of school you belong to, you are a busy person: You're a busy person dedicated to education. Admittedly, there are only so many school hours in the day, and the thought of "fitting in" speech and debate is often daunting to parents, teachers, administrators and students alike.

Actually, *time* is one of the biggest reasons for hesitation. The benefits are obvious – great communication skills, scholarships, friendships, leadership and character building – but we are caught between reaping those benefits and fulfilling other educational commitments.

It may come as a surprise, but these activities can actually *lift* educational burdens. It's easy to judge from the outside looking in: students pouring hours into research, begging to work on their speeches, looking forward to club every week more than any of their other activities. It looks like speech and debate consumes the students!

Ask yourself: *Are these things worthy of complaint?* Speech and debate fits education like a glove, and it actually serves as a conduit for everything educators wish to teach in the first place. Speech and debate hardly takes away from your school work; they *are* your schoolwork.

Those who have been involved for a while know exactly what I'm talking about. Parents and teachers (and especially the students!) begin to realize that this community of training that we call speech and debate is really where our pedagogy should settle. They see the tremendous benefits and are challenged to make speech and debate their paradigm.

Last year some new parents in my club shared their perspective with me. They joined club thinking speech and debate would be a nice "extracurricular" venture. Their son and daughter (both quiet kids, somewhat shy) fell in love with it. They spent a lot of their schooltime studying the philosophical challenges of the Lincoln-Douglas debate topic and working on their oratory speeches. Much of their conversation around the dinner table wasn't about their schoolwork, but about preparation for the next tournament.

"My goodness," my friends first thought. "What about school? This speech and debate stuff is consuming my children! They're not nearly as excited about math and science!"

Then the light turned on. The reality was that they weren't falling behind in any of their work. In fact, as the dad explained to me, "They're learning more than they ever have in their lives!" These parents, like so many I see year after year, began to realize that their complaints were misapplied. Speech and debate became their curricular paradigm, so easy to motivate, and their other curricular studies followed suit.

If you are a student reading this book for a class or because your parents are making you do it, you might as well give up any resistance. You are going to love everything about this activity. You'll learn more than you thought possible, but more so, you'll travel to new places, meet the best of friends, and network with academically focused kids.

Mom and Dad, you are in for the most exciting activity of your children's academic career. Your children are going to grow up and move on in the world. You have them for only a short while. You're already making the sacrifices to provide for them the best education, so I know you are a good parent already. Get involved, don't look back, and watch your kids soar further than you ever imagined possible.

Administrators, be sure you and your school make room for the forensics sport. Budgetary funds should be allocated toward the kids who want to compete in speech and debate, just as much if not more than the school's more noticeable sports activities. In fact, do what you can to make speech and debate popular.

And coach, you are my kindred spirit. Perhaps you don't know a lot about speech and debate, but you know enough to desire to teach it. You know full well the power of thinking, speaking and persuading. The only thing between you and success is a bit of know-how that is in this book.

You made the right choice. Now let's get on to specifics. *Jeub's Guide to Speech & Debate* will guide you through this exciting new adventure of speech and debate.

Organizations

Jeub's Guide to Speech & Debate is specifically tailored to the yearly competitive cycle. Every year is different from the previous (adaptations, new formats, innovated ideas) and families, students and co-ops have to adjust. The change is good, and the activities available are diverse and filled with opportunity.

There are several organizations students can participate in, and an honest analysis of each of these organizations is in order. I'll share with you the organizations I emphasize, but the contents of this book can easily roll into other organizations at your service.

NCFCA

The longest-lasting homeschool speech and debate league is the **National Christian Forensics and Communications Association**, and it's the one that I participated in for 14 years. Started by the Home School Legal Defense Association in 1996, the NCFCA has become one of the largest nationally recognized homeschool extracurricular organizations in the United States. My love for the NCFCA is rooted many years back, and this textbook is specifically tailored to parents and students who desire to get involved in this league.

NCFCA is a league that opens its service to homeschool families nationwide. It is centrally structured and sectioned into 10 geographical regions. Families may "affiliate" with the NCFCA for $55, a $15 discount if completed before September 15, a $15 penalty if completed after December 31. The president governs over regional coordinators, who likewise govern over state coordinators. Speech and debate rules are put together by the league, typically released before the end of the calendar year, and are subject to clarification throughout the school year. State leadership runs **local** or **state tournaments**, while national NCFCA leadership runs individual **regional tournaments** through its 10 regions and a couple of **open tournaments** throughout the year. State tournaments qualify competitors to the state's regional tournament, and the regional and open tournaments qualify competitors directly to the **national tournament**. NCFCA Nationals commences sometime in June, its date and location announced earlier in the year.

Qualifying to **NCFCA Nationals** is possible in the following ways:

1. **Regional Tournaments.** Every region is awarded a certain number of slots to Nationals, and the respected regional tournaments award these slots to the top performers.

2. **Open Tournaments.** These tournaments are open to the entire nation no matter what region a student is from. NCFCA hosts a couple of these in the competitive season after January 1. Top competitors are awarded slots to Nationals.

3. **At-Large Slots.** Each region is allowed a certain number of at-large slots to award to competitors who consistently perform at a high level throughout the year but did not win a slot at regional or open tournaments.

The plans for NCFCA's competitive year are typically announced in the fall or winter months, but that doesn't stop local clubs from planning their tournament schedule. All qualifying tournaments must be sanctioned by the NCFCA, and hosting an open tournament is done by the national leadership. By the end of the calendar year, students and coaches should have a calendar of tournament opportunities within their region where they can apply the skills learned in *Jeub's Guide to Speech & Debate*.

Training Minds hosts speech and debate camps that cater to NCFCA competitors. The publishing house of this book, likewise, publishes other resources for NCFCA families.

There are hundreds (perhaps thousands) of fantastic homeschool families involved in the league. The NCFCA's roots are deep and the rewards for involvement are great. Visit *www.ncfca.org* to find out if there is a coordinator in your area.

Stoa

I live in Colorado, and **Stoa** is the national organization my family participates in, my club is actively involved with, and our state focuses on for the school year. Stoa is not an acronym and is not abbreviated for any longer title. A *stoa* is a classical architectural structure for a porch or public area outside the main structures of an arena. The stoae in Greece and Rome were gathering places for philosophers and citizens to mingle and exchange ideas. Paul's sermon on Mars Hill and his sermon of the unknown god (recorded in the Bible in Acts 16), were given within stoae.

A Stoa membership cost is $40 per family, and coaches with no competing children are able to register as a member for $10. There is a noticeable difference in terminology between Stoa and NCFCA. Families become "affiliates" of NCFCA. Families become a "members" of Stoa. This is a key difference in governance. Stoa is decentralized in governance, allowing states and local clubs to run their own tournaments throughout the year. Stoa's responsibilities are limited to (1) running Stoa's national tournament called the **National Invitational Tournament of Champions (NITOC)**, and (2) creating the qualifying rules for tournament directors and competitors to measure up the coming year of competition to get to NITOC.

NITOC is open to all homeschool speakers and debaters regardless of the league in which they participate. The rules for NITOC qualification are released in August and are not subject to change, even by Stoa's board or committees. There are two types of tournaments that are able to qualify to NITOC: (1) tournaments that include NITOC events, and (2) tournaments that model NITOC itself. Thorough information can be found on Stoa's website, but let me explain the two in brief here:

1. **Regular Tournaments.** Stoa members are able to attend any tournament they wish – in and out of the Stoa organization. When they compete at a tournament that offers the NITOC event, they are able to gain status to qualify to NITOC. It matters not that the tournament is "sanctioned" by Stoa. When students qualify in the event over the course of their competitive year according to Stoa qualifying rules, they receive an invitation to NITOC.

2. **NITOC Modeled Tournaments.** Stoa members who have their sights set on NITOC will want to train to NITOC standards. NITOC Modeled Tournaments will follow the list of guidelines listed on the Stoa website for that year's NITOC tournament. In other words, the rules applied at the end of the year for NITOC will be used at NITOC Modeled Tournaments.

In Stoa, all tournaments are **open tournaments** in that students from other states are able to travel to any tournament they wish (provided there is room at the tournaments). There is no limitation to your attending tournaments based on where you live or even what other league or organization you belong. Stoa tournaments are loaded into the **National Christian Homeschool Speech & Debate Rankings** website *www.speechranks.com*, a Stoa-sponsored database where students are able to track their competitive success. Depending on the points and the number of qualifying checkmarks a student receives, members will receive an invitation to NITOC in April or May.

I had the distinct privilege of running Stoa's 3rd Annual NITOC in Colorado Springs, Colo. in June 2012. NITOC provided competition in 10 individual events, two debate events, and one wild card event. All year long, students tracked their eligibility to NITOC at **SpeechRanks.com**. Invitations to the tournament were calculated on May 1 for the tournament the month later. We hosted 600 students from 28 states in the union, the largest homeschool forensics tournament in its 16 year history.

The same checkmark criteria exists for this year, and will likely continue as long as the place of NITOC is able to withstand the growth. The criteria includes:

- **Two check marks.** Students must perform in their competitive events consistently in a minimum of two tournaments. When students finish a tournament in the top 40% of their event or with a winning record in debate, the student receives a **green check mark** on SpeechRanks.com.

- **Top awarded points.** SpeechRanks.com awards points to students who compete in tournaments based on the size of the tournament and their placing in the tournament.

- **Federalist Awards.** Every state is given at least one invitation to NITOC in each event, no matter the number of checks or points. Most states will have competitors who qualify through the traditional methods listed previously, but states with low involvement are encouraged to come to NITOC through the Federalist Award program.

I suggest that every homeschool speaker and debater become a member of Stoa, even competitors in other leagues. Because if they are unable to receive a qualifying slot from *their* league, they may still be able to clear the merited goals that NITOC requires for the initial April invitations. (Late-comers may still receive an invitation in May, but individual events may be too full to accommodate.)

Stoa offers some exciting innovations for its members. Check out its website for complete information at *www.stoausa.org*.

NFL

The longest-lasting and largest league in America is the National Forensic League (NFL). The NFL offers charter membership to all public and private schools. The league boasts of 120,000 students, 3500 schools and 1.4 million alumni. I'm one of the proud 1.4 million alumni.

The NFL has a clear statement of purpose, located at the top of their homepage of their website:

> *We are the national honor society for secondary and middle school speech and debate. We work to spark transformation in the lives of students, to help them become effective communicators, critical thinkers and engaged, ethical members of our democratic society.*

Membership is done primarily through schools. A public or private school applies for League Membership and are entered in a points system. Students are then given a pin number for their school for which the points they are awarded at tournaments become points affiliated with the member school. A school membership is $99 per year, and each student membership is $15 and lasts a lifetime.

Private educators may sign up as a school just as a public school does. In the eyes of the NFL, home educators may do the same. Though a bit more costly than the Stoa or NCFCA leagues, this is a legitimate option for home educators who wish to join the NFL. Another option would be to join a club at an already-registered NFL school. Check with that school's policy for allowing home educators in their extracurricular functions.

I know many families nationwide who have ventured into the NFL and have prospered. For more information: *www.nationalforensicleague.org*.

Other Organizations

This book focuses mainly on NCFCA, Stoa and NFL. These are the three largest organizations catering to young speakers and debaters, and I am confident that these organizations will maximize the rewards for a student's speech and debate participation. There are, however, others worth mentioning. The following organizations are able to apply the tools in *Jeub's Guide to Speech & Debate:*

- **National High School Mock Trial**. A popular collegiate forensic activity is Moot Court, and a similar high school alterantive is Mock Trial. The title speaks for itself: students compete in a simulated courtroom trial in which they learn about the legal system. Schools host Mock Trial tournaments nationwide that award qualifying opportunities to the national championship. For more information: *www.nationalmocktrial.org.*

- **Christian Communicators of the SouthEast (CCofSE)**. Based in the Carolinas and covering the geographical Southeast, this is a small debate league that formed with a Christian emphasis: "Academically Focused, Christ Centered, Family Oriented." They adopt the Stoa team-policy resolution and write their own public forum debate resolution for the school year. For more information: *www.ccofse.com*

- **Logos Forensics Association (LFA).** The Logos Forensics Association is an alternative to the NFL for private school students. It sprouted up from northern California under the leadership of Michael Winther, a longtime friend of forensics. The association has been slow to grow, but it has opened up tournaments in and out of California. For more information: *www.logosforensics.org*.

- **The Institute for Cultural Communicators (ICC).** Another longtime friend of forensics is Teresa Moon, a founding member of the NCFCA. Her original organization, Communicators for Christ, has branched into the ICC, a broader, more inclusive group that trains homeschoolers, private schoolers, and public schoolers in the arts of communication. For more information: *www.iccinc.org*

To reiterate: Principles from *Jeub's Guide to Speech & Debate* can be utilized in these other leagues and organizations, but the book is written primarily for students, coaches, teachers, administrators and parents in NCFCA, Stoa and NFL. That said, I encourage families to join the organization that best fits their needs. They all offer great benefits to involvement, and as long as the student is speaking and debating, they will reep those benefits.

Resources to Help
Your School's Curriculum

Students, teachers and coaches interested in speech and debate will find the next three chapters dig into the specific events. The leagues come out with their announcements for the following year before the school year begins. For the following year's national tournament, the league will announce new events, changes to previous events, and resolutions for debate topics. *Jeub's Guide to Speech & Debate* will summarize these events in the following chapters, but it is wise to double check with the websites of the league you participate in to make sure you understand the rules of the current competitive season.

Tournaments will have a number of "events" – prepared speech events, limited prep speech events, and debates – for which students can register. By the end of the season, students will know these events very well, as they will observe them in competition. They'll know them *especially* if they compete in them. And after students and teachers understand what is demanded of them for each event, they will construct their education accordingly. They will merge their current curriculum with the demands of their club and upcoming tournaments.

As mentioned, don't be too concerned about speech and debate taking away from other schoolwork. Those who have been involved know how empty this threat is. Students who dive into speech and debate soon become experts in the wealth of education they study, and they typically thrive academically in a host of other areas.

In fact, educators should creatively give credit where credit is due for speech and debate events. Apply a holistic assessment to the topics you're studying in school, and let speech and debate compliment it. If a student is writing a speech on supply-side economics, well, perhaps the economics lesson can be waived. If what needs to be learned can be learned in the preparation for a debate topic rather than a textbook lesson, go with debate. It's a lot more fun and the student will retain the information much better.

This picture was taken at the National Invitational Tournament of Champions.

These debaters competed with one another throughout the week.

Can you think of a better community for young people to be involved in?

The ability to speak in public may be the most important skill to master in life. No wonder it is the scariest.

In This Chapter:

- **Platform Speaking**

    Original Oratory, Expository, Persuasive

- **Literary Interpretation**

    Humorous, Dramatic, Duo

- **Other Speeches**

    Prose, Poetry or Storytelling; Original Interpretation, Open Interpretation, Wildcards

- **Resources**

CHAPTER 2

Speech

All events include some sort of "speech," but when a competitor refers to a "speech event," they typically mean either a platform or literary interpretation event. These two types of speeches are explained in this chapter. A quick definition of these two are:

> **Platform:** *A speech in which the student writes and delivers a speech on a persuasive or informational topic.*

> **Literary Interpretation:** *A speech in which the student reads, interprets and performs a piece of literature.*

For both platform and "interps" (the short term used for literary interpretation), students will learn to really *work* their pieces. Remember, the element of competition is looming ahead of them, and the desire to do well at the next tournament should serve as a proper motivator to keep polishing their work. This is true for all individual events, even limited prep (which we will explore in the next chapter).

Once a speech is selected or written, the student needs to memorize it. Early tournaments may allow students to read a script, but this should be avoided as much as possible. Memorization is an important skill for competitors.

Once memorized, the student has cleared the minimum standard for presenting the speech. It may take some reworking if a student would like to expand the piece or shorten its length. Judges are impressed when speakers hit the maximum allotted time of a speech category, so try your hardest to make that mark. (You'll learn more about times for speeches later in this chapter.)

Now, let's get into what these events actually are. There are several platform and interp events offered in the leagues.

Platform Speaking

Young people naturally desire to express themselves, and a major focus of education should include the opportunity for self-expression within clearly defined guidelines. When a student writes an original speech and delivers it, she is taking a **platform**, hence the name of this type of event. There are several platform categories. Each league has their unique rules and guidelines for proper platform speaking.

Judges rank students on content, organization, rhetoric, delivery and overall impression. All platform speeches are 10 minutes long and students are ranked among a room full of other platform speakers.

Original Oratory

Known as OO, **original oratory** is when the student writes an original speech and delivers it. There are two types of oratory: the **speech to inform** and the **speech to persuade.** OO is considered the broadest type of platform, and though there is an event called "persuasive," OO can include an oratory that is persuasive in nature.

Writing a speech can be fun homework. Instead of sending Junior off to write an ordinary research paper on an event in history, have him write and deliver an interesting speech! If it doesn't inform well, give him coaching tips to improve (versus giving him an F on the paper and sending him back to research). Using a speech to teach will drive your student into learning without him knowing it.

Original oratories can be about objects (the Titanic, race cars, collections, hair styles), people (Patrick Henry, Pocahontas, Martin Luther King Jr., the apostle Paul), events (World War II, Presidential Elections, the signing of the Declaration of Independence), or concepts (how to bake a cake, rebuilding a carburetor). Whatever the student chooses to speak on, her speech can jump-start interest that was not there, or it can be a fueling force behind a preexisting interest.

Original Oratory is an event offered in Stoa and the NFL, not the NCFCA. Instead, the NCFCA offers a unique form of OO called Biographical Narrative. According to the NCFCA, it is still an original oratory, but it "focuses on the relevance and/or contributions of a single person's life." Many of the OO topics listed above fall into the Biographical Narrative category (all the ones surrounding people), but many do not (informative topics or events). These platform topics are covered in other events for NCFCA competitors.

Note that OO is the only platform event offered in the NFL. They are not allowed to use visual aids, just a 10 minute oratory is allowed. Typically the OO is really a persuasive speech, a specific oratory offered in Stoa and NCFCA.

Expository

An **expository** speech, or expos, includes the same purposes as the OO (pretty much whatever the student wants to speak about) but for one aspect: the speaker may use visual aids. Expository speeches are extremely creative speeches that typically use presentation boards on easels as props for the presentation.

Students start creating their expos as an OO. I've coached many students to migrate their OO to an expos, especially if the speech is begging for a visual presentation. The great expository speakers are masters of showing and telling at the same time.

There are some restrictions to expos. According to the Stoa rules:

- The speaker must set up her own props without assistance.

- Clothes or costumes may be put on and used during the speech, but they must not be on the body at the start or end of the speech.

- No weapons, explosives or incendiary devices may be used as visual aids.

- Neither people nor live animals may be used.

- The speaking area must be left in the same condition as it was prior to the speech.

In 2012, Stoa expanded their Expos rules to include electronic equipment for expository speaking. For competition, students are able to incorporate slideshow presentations, as long as the competitor is able to set-up/tear-down during their performance. This alleviates one of the major drawbacks of Expos: the need to transport props from tournament to tournament. It also, in a way, returns to the original purpose of Expos: give a visual representation of the oratory. Professional speakers do that with slideshows nowadays, not boards.

Expos is exclusively a Stoa event, though NCFCA has a more specific form of expos: **Illustrated Oratory (IO)**. The only visual aids allowed in IO are boards, the pieces that affix to the boards and an easel. More specifically:

- **Illustrated Boards.** The number of boards allowed are "3 to 10," according to NCFCA rules. These must measure no larger than 20"x30" (the standard size of store-bought boards). Every speech is required to start and end with a blank board, though it can be the same board.

- **Easel.** Tripod easels can be found at hobby shops and general stores. The easels cannot be modified for the speech other than a ledge for their boards and a visual aid box.

- **Visual Aid Box.** These are handmade boxes attached to the back of the easel. They must have a lid, which must be able to close, thus restricting the size of the visual aids inside. The overall dimensions of the box (length + width + height) must be no larger than 35 inches, about the size of a shoebox. The visual aids retrieved from the box during the presentation may remain attached to the board they are associated with, but must not be showing at the end of the speech.

NCFCA students who follow this protocol will experience the same need to walk the line between *showing* and *telling* as with Stoa's Expos event. The purpose is the same: to present visually the platform speech. The advantage of IO reflects the disadvantage of expos: It is easier to transport the visual aids cross-country (unless they opt for electronic displays only). The disadvantage of IO is the advantage of expos: The creative agility of the speaker is limited by more restrictive display rules.

Persuasive

A speech to persuade is for those students with strong opinions or a fire in their heart to make a change in belief or thought. The power of persuasion is the power to change the world. If anything is needed in today's culture it is the need for strong and *persuasive* leaders.

Aristotle established the ultimate exposé on persuasive speaking in *The Republic*. We learn from him that three necessities in a persuasive speech are *ethos*, *pathos* and *logos*. **Ethos** is the credibility of the speaker, typically the references or appeals to authority that the speaker makes throughout a persuasive speech. **Pathos** is the passion of the speaker, the excitement and the emotion he will inject into his speaking. And then there is **logos**, the logic of it all, the rhetorical connection the speaker makes that reasonably persuades the judge. A mixture of all three makes for the best persuasive speeches.

A **persuasive speech**, alternately referred to as a PS or a pers, must appeal to the *pathos* while upholding a credible *ethos*. Research and documentation are necessary ingredients for a persuasive speaker. We rarely assign a research paper as often as a research speech in our schools. The motivation to research and study the assigned topic is much greater when a speaking event is anticipated by the student.

Literary Interpretation

Literary interpretation students perform a piece of literature for an audience. Students naturally fall in love with stories – fiction, biographies, plays – and will desire to share those stories with others. With interpretation, they have the opportunity to do so. And while they're at it, students will develop their own understanding of the literature and, more significantly, develop skills to communicate the worth of the literature.

There are several types of interpretative speeches, and all the leagues have created their unique presentation formats. I'll get to the differences, but first let me highlight the principles of all literary interpretation speeches.

Students are tasked with creating **scripts** or **manuscripts** from published literature (the only exception being Open or Original Interp where students can use original or unpublished works of literature). Students are not allowed to use one script for more than one year, and a script can only be entered in one event per tournament. Scripts have original word limitations and editing standards, and students need to keep a close eye on the event rules to make sure they are within the guidelines.

- Students are required to submit their scripts physically to the tournament. Both NCFCA and Stoa have guidelines for **script submission** on their websites, and the NFL has guidelines they refer to as **Manuscript Verification Requirements**. Competitors are expected to have their scripts memorized, and judges are instructed to penalize competitors if a physical script is used in the round.

- All the literary interpretation speeches are **capped** at 10 minutes long, no minimum. Judges are given flexibility to that maximum time in case audience participation (like laughter) drags the speech past the limit. The best competitors aim for the 10-minute mark.

- Students are tasked with **cutting** pieces of literature. Cutting requires reading through, then utilizing the cut-and-past tool in a word-processing program to excise parts of the literature to make it suitable for presentation. This must be done without disrespecting the content of the original piece. Guidelines on how to do so are in Travis Herche's excellent book, *Keys to Interp: Breathing Life into Literature* (Monument Publishing), and can also be deciphered in the league rules.

- Students are also tasked with **blocking** their piece. Blocking is the interper's method of acting out the piece. The interper often jumps between narration and character, and perhaps among several characters, too. The rules forbid competitors from using props, and only the speaker's feet are allowed to touch the floor, so the physical challenge of interpers are great (and impressive!). Interpers become masters of the space in the competitive room.

Few of the competitive events are as impressive as the literary interpretive events. Students come alive in front of the judges. If you've never seen one of these events, visit YouTube and do a search for literary interpretations. Some of the recordings will certainly entertain you, and you'll simultaneously get an idea of how to do literary interpretation for competition.

Literature is art, and art can be crafted in ways that puts people off. Competitors sometimes try to push the boundaries of decency, a tactic that doesn't always impress the judges. Bathroom humor or crass jokes aren't shined on in competitions. Likewise, dramatic pieces that shock or are generally inappropriate are discouraged. The best competitors will select pieces that are well written and challenging, avoiding the ones that are inappropriate.

Those are the basics. Now we'll move on to the details of each literary interpretation event.

Humorous

The name speaks for itself: *humorous*. The intent of the **humorous interpretation**, or HI, is to make the audience laugh. This is more than just a rattling off of jokes or standup comedy. Instead, the student will lead the judges through a humorous script.

Dramatic

This name speaks for itself, too: *dramatic*. The intent of the **dramatic interpretation**, or DI, is to tell a dramatic story. The DI is not necessarily void of humor, but the intent isn't to make you laugh. Instead, its purpose is to walk the audience through the drama of a story.

Dramatic is offered in Stoa and NFL, not in NCFCA. However, if an NCFCA student would like to run a dramatic piece, she may do so in open interpretation.

Duo

Duo means what it implies: two competitors speaking together in one speech. All three leagues have their variations of the duo event. The differences are easy to misunderstand, but are significant in preparing for competition.

Duo interpretation (NCFCA and NFL) is just like HI and DI, only done with two people. The duo competitors block their speech to never touch each other or look at each other (as the rules dictate). The duo competitor cuts scripts just like the HI and DI competitors do, the only difference being the dual nature of the presentation.

Duo open (Stoa only) is a new form of duo interp. The rules for duo follow the same strict literary interpretation as HI and DI with rules as to how many original words may be used. Duo open allows speakers the flexibility of the open interp. Pieces may be original and insertions are allowed. Read the rules on Stoa's website for complete information.

Other Speeches

There are quite a few unique forms of other interpretive events that span across the three leagues. They all have the same basic rules (10 minutes of speaking time, can't touch the floor, etc.). You will need to check your league's website for current rules and specifications for these other events, but let's go through a summary of the ones offered now.

Prose, Poetry or Storytelling

These are separate NFL event sometimes run as consolation events at nationals. Some states have opted to merge these events for their local and state tournaments. In any of these events, the students read from the work and are judged on the overall performance of their reading.

Original Interpretation

This is a special event for literary works that the student writes and performs himself. NCFCA exclusively offers this as a yearly competitive event. Students who would like to write their own literary works in Stoa may do so in Open Interp.

Open Interpretation

Open Interp is, as its name suggests, "open" to all sorts of literary works. There is a slight difference between NCFCA and Stoa OI. NCFCA OI competitors may not use original pieces; those pieces would be run in original interpretation. Stoa competitors who wish to run original pieces will need to run them in OI.

Wildcards

A word should be said about "wildcard" events, a special category reserved for a unique event. The NFL calls them "consolation events" and the NCFCA no longer does these, but Stoa has released Wildcard Events for the past two years. In fact, for their 2013 national tournament, they are hosting two wildcard events. Check the leagues' websites for the wildcard/consolation events they're hosting for the next national tournament.

Event	NCFCA	Stoa	NFL
Platform Speaking	Biographical Narrative Illustrated Oratory Persuasive	Original Oratory Expository Persuasive	Original Oratory
Literary Interpretation	Humorous Duo	Humorous Duo Dramatic	Humorous Duo Dramatic
Other	Open Interp Original Interp	Open Interp Original Interp (2012) Storytelling (2013) Mars Hill (2013)	Prose Poetry Storytelling

Resources

There's a lot of detail in all of this. But I hope you're less confused than when you started. I'm in the business of making the confusion *less confusing*. The line of curriculum published by Monument Publishing does just that. And the following list of resources available for you at their website *www.monumentpublishing.com* is designed to help make this an enjoyable activity for you.

We color-coordinate our resources, making it easy to remember what resources go to what event. Speech is labeled as "bronze." The bronze resources are categorized under platforms and interps.

Bronze Book

I have a special fondness for platforms and interps. I believe these speeches serve as a culmination of a strong educational pedagogy more than most other events. These speeches replace term papers all the time in the English classes I teach, and they should. Students still must go through their research and readings, but the adrenaline of preparing a thorough speech for competition elevates the enthusiasm far higher than any school project will.

Our *Bronze Book* (previously published as *Emerald & Platinum* Book) is a collection of model speeches prepared and explained by competition champions. Consider it a fingerprint of a year. Finalists from all leagues are solicited to publish their works in this book, a coil-bound representation of the speeches that made it all the way to the top of their events.

Monument Publishing has been creating this resource since 2010. The idea came from the need for new coaches to have what experienced coaches had: a wealth of examples to draw from. A typical speech coach is able to pull out a file drawer filled with a history of competitive speeches of years past, which is exactly what *Bronze Book* is.

When you own *Bronze Book,* you own the previous year's renditions of the top speeches performed, written or prepared by the competitors themselves. These competitors sometimes have YouTube videos of their performances to give you an idea of their works. Honestly, there is no better way to model champion platform or interp speaking than with the use of *Bronze Book.*

Keys to Interp

Literary interp students have the privilege of a full-fledged textbook, *Keys to Interp: Breathing Life into Literature* by Travis Herche. Travis is the 2006 NCFCA Title Champion of dramatic interp with over a decade of interpretive experience. Travis also competed at the national level in ten individual events, punctuated by an ironman appearance in 2005.

Since then, Travis has coached across the country, helping students to achieve their own success stories. *Keys to Interp* digs deep into the intricacies of good interpretation speaking. It is loaded with advice for serious interpers and comes with discussion questions for larger groups. This textbook is a must-have for every interp student who is dedicated to making the best of their competitive season.

Curriculum

Monument Publishing publishes a large curriculum consisting of five sections of teaching: The Ironman Curriculum. One of the sections is the Bronze section consisting of both platform and literary interpretive speeches. It is a 12-week course that may be diced up to a longer or shorter semester, all meant to prepare the students for speech competition.

This curriculum – as well as the *Bronze Book* itself – is updated yearly and releases before fall semester. You may find these resources at *www.monumentpublishing.com*.

Kasey and Karlyn Leander won 1st place in Duo at the Stoa national tournament in 2012. Their interpretive speech Pinocchio *was the featured speech for the following year's version of Bronze Book.*

Impromptu speaking is much more challenging then you may think. We call it "limited" prep, but there is plenty of preparation needed to make you a champion.

In This Chapter:

- **Impromptu**
- **Extemporaneous**
- **Apologetics**
- **Resources**

CHAPTER 3

Limited Preparation

Students who develop their thinking skills are those who lead in their adult life. They think on their feet, which is a skill virtually everyone wishes they could master. **Limited Preparation** events are for the students who wish to master this skill.

The name does not say it all in this category. For there is a fair amount of preparation required as students get ready for the limited prep event. But the preparation is more practice than it is academic preparedness. That's the part of it that's referenced by "limited preparation," of which there are three individual events – impromptu, extemporaneous and apologetics.

All students are given the equivalent topics for their speaking time. For example, in an impromptu round, all the competitors will be given similar quotes. Or in an extemp round, all students will be given, say, economic questions. The point is for the judges to rate the students fairly in how they present the material. Here is a summary of the criteria judges use in ranking a limited prep event:

1. **Content.** Sure, students are given the topic or question, but how they stick to the topic is just as important. Basic development of thesis,

examples and illustrations reflect on how good a rhetorical speaker they are.

2. **Organization.** Basic understanding of the structure of a speech (introduction, body, conclusion) is ranked here.

3. **Rhetoric.** How succinct are the words of the speech? Does the speech have a fair balance of ethos, pathos and logos?

4. **Delivery.** How good a speaker is the student? The list on one league's impromptu ballot lists energy, vocal clarity, eye contact, authentic style and natural movement.

5. **Overall Impression.** All the limited prep ballots ask for the judge's bottom line impression of the speaker's speech.

Each league has their own layout for limited preparation events, but the idea is the same: *train students to be great impromptu speakers.* Here is a graph of the events offered in each league, and the rest of this chapter goes into detail:

Event Category	NCFCA	Stoa	NFL
Limited Preparation	Impromptu Extemp Apologetics	Impromptu Extemp Apologetics	US Extemp International Extemp

Impromptu

The *American Heritage Dictionary* defines *impromptu* as "something performed or conceived without rehearsal or preparation." An **impromptu** speech is a speech given "off the top of your head." The student is given a creative word or topic and is allowed a limited amount of time to prepare a speech before delivering it. The topic is meant to be specific enough for students to draw from their own general body of knowledge, yet broad enough to allow them to give a strong speech on the topic.

Here's how the competition unfolds: The registered student walks into the room where three judges sit. The judges have been given speech topics when they picked up their ballots (slips of paper placed facedown on the table, or slips of paper in an envelope) and the student draws three. The timekeeper then starts the timer for a two-minute prep time. Two of the three are returned to the judges (or to the table or envelope). The student starts thinking through what she will say following the prep time, sometimes making notes on their own notepaper.

After the prep time is used, the student starts to speak. She must not refer to her notes taken during prep time, only the slip of paper which was provided before the round started. She is given five minutes to speak, and the timekeeper gives hand signals counting the time down. After the speech, the student shakes the hands of the judges and either leaves the room or sits to watch other competitors.

Some tournaments have come up with creative ways to spice up impromptu competition in one round. At the national tournament I ran in 2012, impromptu speakers drew items out of a bag – all obscure medical devices – from which to prepare their impromptu speeches. A tournament in Orange Country I brought my students to had Disney playing cards to select from. Tournaments use all sorts of creative ways to launch the speakers of a particular round into their impromptu speech.

Extemporaneous

Another popular type of limited preparation speaking is **extemporaneous** speaking, popularly referred to as Extemp. Of all the individual events short of debate (which technically is not an individual event), this is likely the most challenging. Instead of just thinking on your feet, the speaker is required to be knowledgeable on current events.

Here, too, a speaker is given a choice of three topics, but he is given 30 minutes to an hour to prepare a seven-minute speech. The extemp draw is done in the extemp prep room at a tournament. The prep room is filled with students researching the topic they chose to speak on. It's a quiet room, overseen by a teacher or coach, where students keep strict track of speaking times and when they are due to take their turn.

Prep rooms are often filled with boxes from extemp clubs whose members spend time filing articles. In recent years, extemp rules in some leagues have allowed computerized filing options for clubs. Online research is not allowed during the tournament preparation. The point of having files ready for competition – either electronically or in print – is one of the educational goals of extemp.

Extemporaneous speaking requires research in current events. The high school student copies articles from popular newsmagazines and news sites and files them (print or electronic) according to topic. This is more time consuming than impromptu, but it keeps the young person up-to-date with what's going on in the world around him. Unlike the normal impromptu speech, the extemporaneous speaker is expected to quote sources from that research.

In Stoa and NCFCA, students are allowed a 3" x 5" index card to keep notes on, but they may go "off card" and deliver by memory. NFL students are required to always go off card. So, in the prep room, students scour the accumulated articles and develop an outline for their speech. They usually have only 30 minutes, but they know they will be ranked based on their background knowledge. Students are allowed to enter the judges' room with only their index card or memory to refer to.

In NFL, students prepare their extemporaneous work into two categories: domestic events (US) and international events. Tournaments separate these into two separate categories, but extemp students typically compete in both. In Stoa and NCFCA, the speech events at a tournament will often select one or the other in a particular round. That is, all students will speak on a domestic topic one round, an international topic the next. Sometimes economic topics will have a mixture of domestic and international.

Extemporaneous speaking may require "limited" preparation at the time of the assignment, but speakers (or "extempers") are not simply spewing words. Nor are extempers reciting carefully worded speeches. Extemp is a cross between impromptu and oratory. Extemporaneous speakers are experts in the topic. They become informed and knowledgeable so much in their studies that when called upon to speak on the topic, they are confident, poised and educated.

Apologetics

The homeschool leagues both have Christian roots, and since 2005 have proposed competitive **apologetics** as a unique limited prep event. Its purpose is to encourage the study and delivery of the fundamentals of the Christian faith. Both the NCFCA and Stoa have 100 or more apologetics questions that relate to Christian doctrine. Judges at tournaments are often pastors or respected people of faith. In Stoa, the apologist is required to address the question as if the audience is not in agreement; NCFCA can assume the audience are believers. These speeches are, at their core, a test of apologia, a defense of the Christian faith.

Here's how it works at a tournament: A competitor will enter a room and choose one of three topics from the judge (as is done in the other limited prep events). The timer will start and the student is allowed four minutes to prepare. Two tools are at the competitor's disposal – a Bible and a personal box with filed cards.

Unlike extemp, the card files must be the individual student's, not a shared box from a club. Students are encouraged to prepare, in their schools, answers to these questions on 4" x 6" note cards that they may refer to during their speech.

Resources

I've been coaching limited prep for years, and the most common mistake students make about limited prep speaking is that it is *no*-prep speaking. There is plenty a limited prep speaker can do to prepare for their speeches. The resources Monument Publishing and Training Minds put out are intended to train the student to be exemplary limited prep competitors.

Gold Book

Monument Publishing and Training Minds has had the privilege of collaborating with the best extemporaneous and impromptu speakers in the country. These competitors have become some of the best coaches in the country, and they head up our Gold line of products.

Cody Herche (2006 NCFCA extemp champion) introduced the *Gold Book* in 2009 as an overview of US, international and economic news. For the novice extemper, the *Gold Book* is invaluable, but is also useful for expert extempers who want to capture an overview of current events. Since 2009, *Gold Book* editors have included other top extemp champion in the homeschool leagues, Shane Baumgardner (2010 and 2011) and Brooke Wade (2012). They all serve as writers for the *Gold Book*.

Here's how the *Gold Book* works. Extemp writers are hired by the editor. This editing group assigns the top news items that extemporaneous speakers must understand. Short articles are written on each topic. Competitors nationwide read these articles to catch up on the current events, sometimes including a print or digital copy for the actual files in their extemp preparation.

Gold Book is not just for extemporaneous speakers. It is wise for all limited prep students to be aware of current events. Debaters – particularly Parli Debaters, as you'll learn about in the next chapter – should pick up a copy of the *Gold Book* to include in their resources. In fact, coaches like me often make the case to our students that the best debaters are extemp speakers, and students typically compete in both events.

Keys to Extemp

Monument Publishing's full-length textbook for the serious extemp speaker is *Keys to Extemp: Speaking From the Heart With the Knowledge in Your Head*. It is written by Cody and is referenced in the Ironman Curriculum. The text explains the details of extemp in much greater detail than this book, and it also gives incredible advice on how to be a champion extemp speaker.

Before *Keys to Extemp* came out in 2008, extemp was not a very popular event. It was seen as exhaustive, so much work that it was not worth the pain. But Cody – with his book and his coaching – has articulated an enthusiasm for the event unlike anyone I have ever seen. Students who follow the principles in *Keys to Extemp* will grow to love the work involved in extemporaneous speaking. And if they're anything like Shane or Brooke, they'll excel to championship levels.

Silver Book

Apologetics is vast and wide, allowing for a myriad of options for students to jump into. Training Minds Ministry and Monument Publishing have been blessed with some outstanding coaches that are masters at simplifying the immensity, and they have preselected great sources from which to start.

Apologetics competitors need to get the *Silver Book,* written by Luis Garcia and Cynthia Jeub. There are two editions to the *Silver Book*: the Stoa and the NCFCA editions. Both leagues have unique questions from one another, and each edition prepares students to answer these questions.

Luis and Cynthia refer to many resources throughout the *Silver Book.* References to the Bible are included in every topic. They also reference historically significant theologians like C.S. Lewis. Also included in *Silver Book* are modern apologists. Monument Publishing provides additional resources in a package that includes *Silver Book.*

Curriculum

The Ironman Curriculum is the all-inclusive curriculum mentioned earlier, and two of the five sections cover limited prep events extemp and apologetics. The curriculum is set up as Gold (extemp) and Silver (apologetics) and cover 12 weeks of lessons for each discipline.

These resources are updated yearly and are available in time for the new school year to start. You may find these resources at *www.monumentpublishing.com*.

Shane Baumgardner is a Training Minds alumnus, pictured here holding his many trophies at nationals. He is the only student in the country to own two titles in impromptu from two different leagues, Stoa and NCFCA. He is currently a law student at the University of Minnesota, one of the youngest ever to attend their program.

Can you tell I'm proud of him? Speech and debate champions go far in life.

Not brute force, but only persuasion and faith are the kings of this world.

~ Tomas Carlyle

In This Chapter:

- **Team-Policy**
- **Lincoln-Douglas**
- **Public Forum**
- **Parliamentary**
- **Resources**

CHAPTER 4

Debate

My heart goes out to the beginning debater, especially the beginning parent or coach of a debater. Debate is an entire sport full of rules, new terminology, and a host of jargon to go along with it. Wading through the how-to's is enough to scare off the most determined individual. But hang in there! Debate may be the most rigorous academic activity out there, but it is also the most rewarding. Students – even the most academically challenged – eventually get it and enjoy it.

Debate is much like American football to a European. "Football" to a European is padless joggers kicking a checkered ball around the field. What does a Manchester United fan know of touchdowns, touchbacks, field goals, blitzes, offsides, clipping, facemasks, interference, 15-yard penalties or extra points (either 1 or 2)? Following the NFL (the National Football League, that is) for the uninitiated is like trying to understand a foreign language!

Only when the game is *understood* does it become *enjoyable.* Football fans enjoy arguing over calls, discussing game strategies, debating draft picks. There is so much culture intertwined in the American sport of football that people from the outside usually throw up their hands, thinking Americans are almost cultish in their frenzy.

I have had the opportunity to teach and coach many debaters. My curriculum always includes time for lengthy class sessions in which I teach the basics of academic debate. Sometimes the students get frustrated at the complexities; sometimes they want to quit. But once they get the chance to jump into a round at their first debate competition, the pieces fall into place. They see their studies pay off and find it to be a lot of fun!

There is an entire language and rapport in the sport of debate. It may seem foreign at first, but don't panic! Once you see a few rounds, study up on the topic and give it a try for yourself, you'll soon fall into an understanding that will bring great reward.

There are several types of debate available to students, varying from league to league. Each has a unique topic for the semester or season, often for the entire competitive year. And each format offers a unique skill set. A *resolution* is the league-approved topic laid out in a carefully worded statement. The resolution is what kicks off every debate round at every tournament in every league.

While there are many debate formats, I cover the four most popular formats offered in junior high and high school: *Team-Policy, Lincoln-Douglas, Public Forum* and *Parliamentary.* Let's get our brains around what each debate event requires.

Team-Policy

I've been coaching team-policy debate, also referred to by the initials TP or TD (for team debate), since 1995. It is my pleasure to judge TP, coach TP and watch TP. It is the most demanding event of any league. So it's worth our time here to take apart the two words of TP and explain each of them.

Team

Team means that debate teams consist of two debaters each. A TP round is 2-on-2. The debaters enter the room knowing which speeches they will run and will have trained for a division of labor between them. Here is a rundown of responsibilities between the two sides, and an explanation of the duties for each speech:

1. **First Affirmative Constructive (1AC)** - 8 min.
   The 1A gives a prepared eight-minute speech presenting his case to the judge. This is followed with a three-minute cross-examination by the 2N.

2. **First Negative Constructive (1NC)** - 8 min.
   The 1N addresses much of the 1A's case within the eight-minute timeframe. This is followed with a three-minute cross-examination by the 1A.

3. **Second Affirmative Constructive (2AC)** - 8 min.
   The 2A refutes the 1N's speech within eight minutes. This is followed with a three-minute cross-examination by the 1N.

4. **Second Negative Constructive (2NC)** - 8 min.
   The 2N runs various arguments against the affirmative case. This is followed with a three-minute cross-examination by the 2A.

5. **First Negative Rebuttal (1NR)** - 5 min.
   The 1N gives a five-minute rebuttal primarily to the 2AC.

6. **First Affirmative Rebuttal (1AR)** - 5 min.
   The 1A gives a five-minute rebuttal to the two previous negative speeches.

7. **Second Negative Rebuttal (2NR)** - 5 min.
   The 2N sums up the round and urges a negative ballot.

8. **Second Affirmative Rebuttal (2AR)** - 5 min.
   The 2A sums up the round and urges an affirmative ballot.

It seems complicated, especially if you're new to this. But that stress will melt away when you watch it work and get used to the even exchange of ideas. Monument Publishing's *Blue Book* is helpful here, too, as it walks the debater through the demands of the speakers.

In summary, notice the following things in the typical 90-minute debate round:

- The affirmative team speaks first and last. This is because the affirmative team has what's called the **burden of proof**. They must convince the judge to change the **status quo**. The negative team rests with **presumption**, meaning that if the affirmative fails to uphold their burden of proof, the negative should win. Of course, this is debate theory (there is no rule that states this must exist in every round), but it helps us understand why the affirmative has the first and last word in the round.

- The negative team has 13 minutes of speaking time in the middle (speeches 4 and 5), right next to each other. This is called the **negative block**, and it is a strategy for negative debaters to split the responsibilities between the two speeches.

- The debate round is divided into two parts: the **constructives** and the **rebuttals.** The names reflect what happens. The constructive speeches build arguments, and the rebuttals simply refute what the constructives bring up. New arguments should not appear in the rebuttals.

- The **cross-examinations**, also called CX or cross-X, are the most fun parts of the round. They take place in the constructives, but they should not be confused with the speeches. Debaters should not make arguments in CX, but should carry the **admissions** in the CX to their speeches.

Policy

Policy refers to the type of resolution the debaters will be debating. The resolutions are political in nature. Every year the homeschool organizations switch between foreign and domestic issues. The National Forensic League does not necessarily revolve the two. All three leagues have their current team-policy topics listed on their websites.

Here is a list of resolutions of past years, a sampling from every league:

- NFL 1996 – Resolved: That the federal government should establish a program to substantially reduce juvenile crime in the United States.

- NFL 2002 – Resolved: That the United States federal government should substantially increase public health services for mental health care in the United States.

- NFL 2013 – Resolved: The United States federal government should substantially increase its transportation infrastructure investment in the United States.

- NCFCA 1997 – Resolved: That the United States should change its rules governing foreign military intervention.

- NCFCA 2006 – Resolved: That the North Atlantic Treaty Organization (NATO) should be significantly reformed or abolished.

- NCFCA 2012 – Resolved: The United States Federal Government should significantly reform its criminal justice system.

- Stoa 2012 – Resolved: That the United States federal government should substantially reform its revenue generation policies.

- Stoa 2013 – Resolved: The United States Federal Government should substantially reform its foreign military presence and/or foreign military commitments.

It is important to note that the league resolutions are specific to the year of debate for members of the leagues. Most other debate formats change throughout the year. This is likely because of the amount of research team-policy debate requires. Leagues enjoy choosing one topic area – defined by the resolution – to which the debate teams study all year long, all the way up to their national tournaments.

"Blue" = Team-Policy Debate

Stepping into the resolutions takes up an entire book in and of itself, and that book is the already-mentioned *Blue Book*. It's a great resource (if I do say so myself) that I've published every year since 1998, and it's currently a research-and-writing collaboration between my co-author, Vance Trefethen, and myself. I encourage all debaters to get a copy.

We currently publish two editions: *Stoa* and *NCFCA*. Each is published with introductory chapters designed to help students learn and grow in their debate ventures, especially novices trying to figure out the ins and outs of team debate. Debaters are also given case extensions and briefs, ready to run in a debate round.

Here's how it works: Team-policy debaters will order the *Blue Book* in the edition relevant to their competition plans. The book will serve as an introduction to the resolution and will include 12 foundational cases meant for kicking off the year. A midseason supplement is released on January 1 of the competitive year, strategically placed before the first tournaments.

We do not currently publish a *Blue Book* for the NFL, but there are a host of other sourcebook publishers for team-policy debaters into that market. See the National Forensic League's website for more information.

All this to say: *sourcebooks help tremendously*. They're not substitutes for good debating, but having the model to follow in *Blue Book* makes for an enjoyable and successful debate year.

Lincoln-Douglas

Lincoln-Douglas, or LD, debate is named after the famous 19th century debates between Abraham Lincoln and Stephen Douglas. The two traveled the state of Illinois and debated the heated political issues of the day while racing for the Illinois senate seat. History shows that debate isn't all about winning rounds. Lincoln lost to Douglas in the senate race, but the skills learned during the process helped galvanize his run for the presidency.

If you think LD is just a scaled down version of TP, think again. The event is sharply different in structure and approach.

One-on-One Format

LD debates are one-on-one timed sessions over the course of approximately 45 minutes. Here's how the round unfolds:

1. **Affirmative Constructive (AC)** - 6 min.
    The affirmative gives a prepared six-minute speech presenting her case to the judge. This is followed with a three-minute cross-examination.

2. **Negative Constructive (NC) + First Negative rebuttal (1NR)** - 7 min.
    The negative builds a case of his own within the seven-minute timeframe, but also leaves time to rebut the affirmative's case. This is followed with a three-minute cross-examination by the affirmative.

3. **First Affirmative Rebuttal (1AR)** - 4 min.
    The affirmative refutes the negative's speech within four minutes.

4. **Second Negative Rebuttal (2NR)** - 6 min.
    The negative refutes the affirmative's speech within six minutes.

5. **Second Affirmative Rebuttal (2AR)** - 3 min.
    The affirmative has the last word on the debate within three minutes.

This structure has to be, of course, different from team-policy since this is one-on-one debate. But there are some similarities. First, each speaker gets the same amount of speaking time and the affirmative gets the first and last word. Both sides get to lead (ask) and follow (answer) cross-examination.

The stark difference between team-policy and Lincoln-Douglas is the kind of debate it is. Lincoln-Douglas debate is "value" debate: philosophical in nature, not political. Students are tasked to analyze the resolution within the framework of a value. Furthermore, each side (affirmative and negative) carry a burden of proof to show how their value best upholds the resolution. There is no presumption in value debate.

Values

As already noted, LD is *value* debate, different from *policy* debate. Policy debaters argue over the same sorts of topics as politicians, while value debaters argue more as philosophers. Policy is concerned over what course of action is better or worse, while value is concerned over what is right or wrong.

The Stoa and NCFCA debate leagues run one value resolution per year while the NFL runs four. All tournaments falling within the timeframe of the released resolution argue these topics all the way up to the leagues' national tournament (the NFL adopts its 4th resolution for the national tournament). You may see the current resolutions posted on the individual leagues' websites.

For reference sake, here are some sample LD resolutions of the past:

- NFL 2008: Resolved: In a democratic society, felons ought to retain the right to vote.

- NFL 1998: Resolved: civil disobedience is justifed in a democracy.

- NCFCA 2003: Resolved: That human rights should be valued above national sovereignty.

- NCFCA 2007: Resolved: Democracy is overvalued by the United States government.

- Stoa and NCFCA 2010: Resolved: That competition is superior to cooperation as a means of achieving excellence.

- Stoa 2013: Resolved: Privacy is undervalued

"Red" = Lincoln-Douglas Debate

Since 2001 Monument Publishing has published a sourcebook for Lincoln-Douglas debaters called the *Red Book.* Today it is written by champion LD competitors and coaches. Since there are *sides* to the resolutions rather than "presumptions," the *Red Book* consists of papers of philosophical positions along with sample cases. These cases can sometimes be run on either side of the resolution.

The editor of the *Red Book* heads up a writing staff of other champions. They write philosophical papers and sample cases meant to lead the LD debater through analysis of the resolution. Read up on the biographies of the *Red Book* authors on the Training Minds authors page. You'll be impressed! So impressed that you'll want to have the *Red Book* if you're going to be a Lincoln-Douglas debater.

Like *Blue Book,* the *Red Book* is currently published for the Stoa and NCFCA leagues only, each with its own edition. They release at the beginning of every year. For NFL debaters, there are sourcebooks available elsewhere. Also, research the archives of Monument Publishing's *Red Books.* It may just happen that the resolution for your semester has a *Red Book* just for you.

Lincoln-Douglas debate is an excellent format for philosophically minded students. We've covered the demands of the competitor here in a nutshell. The *Red Book* carries the debater through to become a champion.

Public Forum

Public Forum Debate, also referred to as "crossfire" debate, is a form of debate that incorporates much of the same features of team-policy explained above. It is solely used in the National Forensic League (not in NCFCA or Stoa), seen as a milder form of TP, and has grown to be one of the most popular forms of public school debate.

The resolutions for Public Forum debate are released every month. Debaters prepare to speak on either the pro (affirmative) or con (negative) side. The topics chosen are policy resolutions that, as with extemp, are politically hot topics at the time. There is no cross-examination, but rather "crossfire," meaning debaters are allowed the chance to ask each other questions (rather than one side cross-examining the other).

The timed format for Public Forum is as follows:

1. **Team A:** First Speaker: Constructive Speech - 4 min.

2. **Team B:** First Speaker, Constructive Speech - 4 min.
   Crossfire between the first two speakers - 3 min.

3. **Team A:** Second Speaker, Rebuttal - 4 min.

4. **Team B:** Second Speaker, Rebuttal - 4 min.
   Crossfire between the second two speakers - 3 min.

5. **Team A:** First Speaker, Summary - 2 min.

6. **Team B:** First Speaker, Summary - 2 min.
   Grand crossfire including all speakers - 3 min.

7. **Team A:** Second Speaker, Final Focus - 2 min.

8. **Team B:** Second Speaker, Final Focus - 2 min.

Public Forum was an answer to what had become known as "speed debate" in team-policy debate. Speed debate consists of debaters speaking so fast that only trained debate judges were able to follow along the arguments with any understanding. The NFL typically hires college debaters or previous debaters to judge policy rounds at their tournaments. The homeschool leagues (NCFCA and Stoa) depend on parent and community judges, so team-policy debaters aren't advised to practice "speed."

Unlike team-policy, Public Forum has a current event flavor much similar to extemp (discussed in the last chapter) or parli (discussed in the next section). This is because resolutions change every month, and the NFL enjoys writing resolutions based off top stories in the news. Here are past resolutions:

- December 2007: "Resolved: That the United States would be justified in pursuing military options against Iran."

- December 2008: "Resolved: That, on balance, social networking Web sites have had a positive impact on the United States."

- September 2009: Resolved: United States policy on illegal immigration should focus on attrition through enforcement rather than amnesty.

- January 2010: Resolved: President Obama's plan for increasing troops in Afghanistan is in the United States' best interest.

- September 2011: Resolved: The benefits of post-9/11 security measures outweigh the harms to personal freedom.

- September 2012: Resolved: Congress should renew the Federal Assault Weapons Ban.

If you know recent history of current events well, you'll see that these resolutions are on topics that students may (or should) have known about. Same with the judges. Public Forum is a fun format for debate.

Parliamentary

Parliamentary debate, or parli, as it's often called, has been run for years in collegiate debate. It has made its debut in the homeschool leagues in certain areas and has been adopted as an official event in Stoa. Like public forum, parliamentary debate mixes formal debate up a little, giving debaters the opportunity to interrupt each other, ask questions, and even give shout-outs during the debate.

The format of parli is so unique that it is difficult to run as a speech event or another debate event. This shouldn't intimidate competitors. Quite the contrary, parli is very simple to run on its own. Here are some bullet points on how parli works.

- Parli involves advanced skill sets, recommended only for 16- to 18-year-old competitors. Younger students are allowed to compete with coach approval, but keep in mind that these students should first have a grasp of value and policy debate already.

- Resolutions are different every round, and they are different in structure. Resolutions may be policy, value, or even fact. Tournament directors write these resolutions specifically for their tournament.

- These resolutions are announced 15 minutes before the round begins. Students are dismissed to prepare for their rounds as either the government (affirmative) or the opposition (negative).

- Internet access, computer use, conversations with coaches, and use of any pre-tournament preparation are allowed in the 15 minutes of prep time. Prep time closely resembles extemp prep rooms, but students are able to converse and prepare as they see fit.

- Parli speeches are limited prep speeches. Students appeal to general knowledge and a broad perspective of current events or philosophy rather than cited evidence as proof of positions.

- There is no preparation time allowed in parli rounds. Interruptions are allowed in the form of questions, much like cross-examinations in TP and LD, called "points of information." Debaters may also make "points of order" that are like objections to a formality of the round.

- Respectful audience participation is encouraged. Knocking on tables or chairs as good points are made, or a "Hear! Hear!" is not uncommon.

- It is very possible for a debater to continue debating in TP or LD and also compete in parli. The preparation is similar to extemp. In fact, most parli debaters are also competitors in TP or LD.

I'm personally excited about parli debate for a number of reasons. First, it provides an educational debate using open-book research. Second, parli is an advanced debate of sorts, requiring only experienced or older debaters into the format. Third, parli brings both value and policy debate together (and sometimes fact) for a well-rounded educational experience.

Being such a new event, there isn't a dedicated Monument Publishing parli resource, but I'm not sure there needs to be one. Parli speakers are experts at current events, just like an extemper. *Gold Book* products will work perfectly for the parli debater. For more information on how to fit parli into your competitive schedule, visit *www.stoausa.org*.

Resources

As I stated at the beginning of the chapter, debate vocabulary is like a foreign language. I cannot imagine getting along without the help of some punctual resources.

Sourcebooks

As already mentioned, the *Blue Book* and the *Red Book* are excellent sourcebooks for debaters participating in Team-Policy and Lincoln-Douglas debate. They each come with thorough explanations of the resolutions the debaters will learn to master, a kick-off for the year that is unquestionably helpful. In fact, these sourcebooks are Monument Publishing's bestselling resources.

I strongly encourage coaches – both new and old – to use the *Blue Book* and *Red Book* as their main resource when teaching these formats of debate. I've known coaches who refuse to adopt them – citing some nonsense about how they are somehow cheating the educational value of debate – and these coaches eventually grow frustrated. Either they grow tired of reinventing the entire discussion around the topic, or they grow tired of seeing their teams get defeated at tournaments.

Because topics change so often with Public Forum, NFL Lincoln-Douglas, and especially Parli Debate, Monument Publishing does not publish a sourcebook for these formats. However, the *Gold Book* is becoming the popular book to get for students. As explained in the last chapter, the *Gold Book* covers the most important current events for extemporaneous speakers. And extemp is, of course, what all debaters must do naturally.

In summary, the sourcebooks to get are:

- Team-Policy: *Blue Book*

- Lincoln-Douglas: *Red Book*

- Public Forum and Parli: *Gold Book*

Flowsheets

"Flowing" a debate round is the note-taking process debaters do during the debate round. Judges, too, often adopt flowing to keep track of the arguments presented in a round. Flowing is perhaps the most important skill to master as a new debater. In fact, we have at our debate camps a simple motto: "You gotta flow every time. That, my friend, is the bottom line."

Monument Publishing produces a coil-bound collection of Training Minds Flowsheets. Debaters are able to keep their flows together (rather than in a messy pile) for discussion in club, with other debaters, with parents, and so on. These flowsheets are a record of the actual round.

Curriculum

Previous chapters explain academic speech. Coaches with a good sense about them can get by with training new speakers in competition simply by reading the rules. Debate is a whole other game, and a formal curriculum is really what is needed.

Included in the Ironman Curriculum are two 12-week courses written by two coaches, Jesse Byrnes (Lincoln-Douglas) and myself (Team-Policy). These are for people who are searching for a deeper understanding of these two popular formats of debate.

You can find all these resources at *www.monumentpublishing.com*. There are more resources for debaters that we'll cover later in the book. First, let's talk a bit about the end result of hard classroom work, the tournaments!

Tournaments create memories of a healthy educational heritage.

In This Chapter:

- **Calendar**
- **Script Submission**
- **Ethical Evidence**
- **Read the Rules**
- **Adjudication**
- **Registration Deadlines**
- **Judging Requirements**
- **Family**

CHAPTER 5

Tournaments

If you've never attended a tournament, you are in for a rush. They can be the most fun events in students' lives, as well as the chance for them to stretch their competitive muscles. Depending on where you live, you may have a robust schedule of tournaments to choose from. If not, there are several opportunities to travel outside your area. Any which way you slice it, students are able to connect with other students and form friendships that will last a lifetime through speech and debate.

There are a number of important expectations competitors should have to help prepare for competition.

Calendar

Whether you are a coach, a parent, administrator or a competitor, gearing up for a year of speech and debate competition is a year-round process. Sure, the tournament season lasts only a few months. But to fully capture the spirit of the competition and reap its full rewards, you will make it a point to plan ahead and get involved.

Here's a typical year in preview:

- Summer: Go to speech and debate camp.
- September-December: Go through curriculum with a school, co-op, a club or individual study.
- January-April: Tournament season.
- May-June: Nationals.

Script Submission

All three leagues require script submission before the tournament begins. NCFCA and Stoa tournaments refer to it as **script submission,** and the NFL refers to it as **manuscript verification requirements**. This is to help tournament directors quickly solve rules violations. If a judge or other competitor raises an issue during the tournament, officials will pull the script and review it to validate the claim.

Script submission guidelines are for all platform and interpretive speeches. Cover sheets and instructions are available on the leagues' respective websites. Students are to print the cover sheets, their required documents and works-cited pages. I don't exhaust the details of script submission in this book, so be sure to visit the websites for complete up-to-date information.

A pre-tournament option is **electronic script submission**. Quite a few tournaments established an e-process where students email or upload the required documents. This helps speed up the process and avoid long lines at check-in.

Ethical Evidence

Debaters – particularly team-policy debaters – must have evidence printed and properly cited before submitting it into a debate round. Students sometimes get themselves into trouble when their citations do not measure up and their opposing team raises an **ethical violation**. Most often when evidence issues are brought up, sloppiness is the case. However, it is never justified to have tampered-with or fabricated evidence in the round, sloppy or not, and teams can be disqualified for it.

The *Blue Book* goes into great detail for the team-policy debaters on how to properly cite evidence, what is or isn't legitimate, and how to sniff out the foul play of opponents. Lincoln-Douglas or parliamentary debaters don't need to wrestle with this issue much, but ethical debaters do.

Read the Rules

Any law enforcement officer knows the most common excuse from lawbreakers: "I didn't know." This is not an excuse for breaking the law, and neither is it an excuse to break the **rules** of speech and debate. When called on the carpet, students and coaches should be prepared to defend their actions. Speech and debate is a competitive sport, and everyone is expected to play within the rules. Ignorance is not a free pass to break them.

We make it a club practice to read the rules together (all leagues have downloadable documents available) and we answer all associated questions.

Adjudication

Individual success relies on the expectation that others are playing within the rules. So when speakers or debaters are suspected of breaking one (intentionally or not), an **adjudication team** is assembled to investigate. This usually consists of area coaches or tournament staff who are respected leaders in the community.

There is no set rule on how adjudication committees ought to run. I've seen healthy and unhealthy adjudication over the years, and have served on many different committees. Every issue will bring its own unique flavor to the adjudication team, but these steps have helped in making sure the issues are taken care of and people are handled with respect.

1. The Tournament Director, or TD, gathers the information about the infraction from the person making the complaint. The TD has the choice to either handle it on the spot (which solves the issue) or assemble the adjudication committee.

2. The TD relates the situation to the committee, but keeps names as anonymous as possible. This is fact-finding time as the adults in the room try to figure out the truth.

3. The committee runs through scenarios on how to handle the adjudication. Serious infractions lead to turned ballots or forfeiture, less serious turn into talks with coaches and a learning situation.

4. The committee either meets with the student or coach, or a person is assigned to take care of the situation. For more serious situations, the tabulation room is notified of any changes that need to take place.

5. The tournament returns quickly to schedule.

A goal of adjudication is to handle the problem as quickly and fairly as possible so that the tournament can continue on track. Warning: Adjudication committees that fish for intent rarely come out ahead. Stick to the rules and avoid deciphering theory or nuances. A common practice in proper tournament administration is for the TD to open up the rule book and ask, "What rule was broken?" If a rule cannot be pointed to, then adjudication is usually not needed.

Registration Deadlines

Tournaments have two dates: "open" dates for registration and "closing" dates. Don't assume the tournament will have slots for long. Popular tournaments have been known to fill up within a day or two – maybe even hours. For those tournaments you want to get into, make sure you are at your computer ready to register when the tournament is scheduled to open.

Connor McKay is a former student of mine who developed **FlowPro**, a registration system that many tournament directors use to set up their tournament registration. The first page of tournaments using FlowPro has all the necessary information for tournament, and sub-pages are listed on the navigation bar. All FlowPro websites are easy to manage and registration is easy to do. You can find out more at _www.homeschooldebate.net_.

Judging Requirements

Depending on the number of events you enter, you will be required to bring judges to your tournament. They will not judge you, of course (that would be a conflict of interest), but they are needed to keep a tournament rolling along. There are three kinds of judges at tournaments.

1. **Parent Judges.** These are moms and dads of competitors. Most often competitors register their parents for judging when they are registering themselves for a tournament.

2. **Alumni Judges.** These are students who have graduated and are at least 18 years old. Tournaments scheduled during spring breaks typically draw several alumni judges.

3. **Community Judges.** These are judges who are not parents or alumni. These could include grandparents or relatives of competitors, co-workers of parents, friends, neighbors and the like.

The first two types of judges are pretty common at tournaments, but all tournaments need a pool of community judges to succeed. Students are encouraged to solicit community judges and are sometimes awarded prizes for their efforts. I can't emphasize enough the importance of a healthy community judge pool. Tournament organizers should treat community judges like royalty (thank them often and feed them well), because they want them to return.

Family

Competitors aren't the only ones to enjoy one another at tournaments. Here are ways other family members can be of service _and_ have a great time too.

- **Timers**. Children 9-11 years old (not yet old enough to compete) can time rounds. The timer table is a popular area at tournaments. NFL judges are typically required to time as well as judge, but they are welcome to bring a smaller child to do the job for them.

- **Judges.** What better way to get relatives involved than judging at a speech and debate tournament?

- **Staff.** Families can pitch in by overseeing or helping with facilities work, orientation, way-finding, etc. It always ends up being more fun than drudgery, and we have had parents enjoy staffing tournaments even after their own kids have graduated and moved on to college-level debate.

You will find that tournaments are exhausting, but *so totally worth it*. Speech and debate enthusiasts form a wonderful hub of community. Friendships formed at these tournaments will last a lifetime.

These beautiful trophies were put together in Colorado.
Unique stones mined from the Rocky Mountains,
students from across the country brought them home.

Tournaments build community.
Though tournaments are competitive,
they bring people together.

In This Chapter:

- **Camp**
- **Coaching**
- **Curriculum**
- **Commitment**

Successful competitors give attention to "training for action" with camp, coaching, curriculum and commitment.

CHAPTER 6

The C's to Success

What turns the "good" competitor into a "great" competitor? What helps get a student on the top of the charts? What can *you* do to fully engage in the competitive arena and stay ahead of the rest?

Don't settle for mediocrity. The masses settle there, but the great communicators and leaders of the future climb up to higher ground. The competitive environment encourages you to press yourself, to strive for greatness. This isn't a haughty or proud attitude – blow that thought away. Striving for greatness in all you do is a noble goal indeed.

I have found four C's to a students speech and debate success. They are:

- Camp

- Coaching

- Curriculum

- Commitment

This chapter is about these four C's and what exactly you can do to best prepare for the action of upcoming tournaments. Let me lay out these opportunities so you can take full advantage of this school year.

Camp

Training Minds hosts camps which I lead. I hire Training Minds coaches to do the good work of coaxing the most and the best out of the campers. I try to find venues that motivate students to maximize their learning potential, and often entire clubs and families attend. By all means, come!

I know what you're thinking right now, though! "I probably can't afford this." There are two ways we help make this happen. First, we offer some incredible deals. Camp isn't as expensive as you might think. Check out the Training Minds website to get a good idea of what kind of deals we have to offer at next year's speech and debate camps.

Second, Training Minds is able to accept tax-deductible donations with requests for the funds to go to attending students. This means that campers can solicit friends, families and businesses for donations to raise money for camp. The process follows IRS guidelines and has been an incredible opportunity to make camp affordable. In the past five years, over $40,000 in contributions has been raised for camp tuition.

My bottom line is this: *I don't want anyone to turn away from camp because of finances.* Anything is possible, right? If you have the will, you can find the way. Training Minds is ready to work with you to make it happen. Spend some time on our website looking over the deals that are offered, and contact us if you need to talk through your particular situation.

Still, if you aren't able to make it to camp, Monument Publishing produces some extensive materials for self-study. We record some of the sessions at camp and produce sets of CDs and DVDs. A good use of time would be to work through the lessons in the audio and video sets.

Coaching

I've been coaching since 1995 and will continue to coach for years to come. I can't get enough of it! But nearly 20 years into this, Training Minds has better coaches on the roster than me. So while I don't personally boast that I'm the best there is, I can boast that *we* have the best coaches in the nation at our camps and making resources for publication. And we're having a ball doing it!

Getting **coaching support** is a difficult thing sometimes. But it isn't impossible. A few dedicated educators scoping the local area could turn up some fabulous speech and debate coaching. Here are some suggestions:

- **Colleges.** If you live close to a college, try to find out if it has a forensics department. I've seen some marvelous coaches come from collegiate circles.

- **Alumni.** They've walked the walk, so why not pull them in to talk the talk? Invite your graduates to come back to club and coach the next generation of students. If they're heading out of town for college, set up times for when they're back in town for "special sessions" of coaching.

- **Mom and/or Dad.** There is nothing wrong with parents learning alongside students. I know many coaches – some with teams that have done extremely well in national competition – who started out as ambitious parents. They started knowing perhaps no more than you holding this book, and they fared very well in the long run.

- **Coaching Brokering System.** Training Minds brokers our fine coaches. What that means is this: Our coaches are open to being contracted to help individual students and even entire clubs. Get more information about this venture by visiting *www.trainingminds.org/coaches*.

Don't get discouraged if none of these things happen. Students who have ambition and teach one another sometimes do nicely. It may take a while to build a club with mature coaching support. That's not the end of the world. Do what you can, and watch your club grow.

Curriculum

A tournament "ironman" is a competitor who competes in five speaking events and debate. She is often given a special award for such enthusiasm and dedication.

Now, I'm not saying that everyone in your club must or even should be ironmen. However, it is good to be exposed to all the speech and debate categories sometime during middle school and high school. This is the purpose of the *Ironman Curriculum*.

I've mentioned the *Ironman Curriculum* here and there in previous chapters. This is Monument Publishing's all-inclusive, quite hefty three-ring binder of lessons for each speaking event.

The curriculum releases every year in August and is made for coaches seeking supplemental material to teach their students. Even so, some mature, established coaches have gone with this material which is written by Training Minds coaches and can be easily adapted to the classroom or co-op setting.

The *Ironman Curriculum* consists of five 12-week sessions specifically tailored for students who desire to excel in any of the speeches offered in the various leagues. The lessons may be purchased separately too. The idea of the *Ironman Curriculum* is to teach *everything* a students needs to know to become an ironman competitor at a tournament. Naturally, students won't participate in all the events, but they will at least be exposed to their details in case they would like to pursue them for competition.

We publish the syllabi online for coaches to copy and use as they wish. The syllabi may be used as is or adjusted to fit a club's needs. The links to the syllabi can be found on the *Ironman Curriculum* product page: *www.monumentpublishing.com/ironman.*

Sourcebooks & Textbooks

I've covered sourcebooks in earlier chapters, so I won't spend too much time on them here. In short:

- "Blue" = Team-Policy Debate

- "Red" = Lincoln-Douglas Debate

- "Gold" = Extemp, Impromptu & Parli Debate

- "Silver" = Apologetics

- "Bronze" = Literary Interp and Platforms

Sourcebooks are coil-bound study helps, not quite the year-by-year textbook that students can also find handy. We have developed quite a collection of foundational texts for students and coaches to learn from. They are *"Keys"* to ensuring the best practices for each discipline.

Keys is the title of our line products, and we hope to make more in the future. Unlike sourcebooks, textbooks may be used year to year and do not come out with new editions very often. These are the ones that have already been released or are to be released this year.

- *Keys to Extemp* by Cody Herche (2008)

- *Keys to Interp* by Travis Herche (2010)

- *Keys to Cross-Examination* by Cody Herche (2011)

- *Keys to Team-Policy* by Vance Trefethen (2012)

- *Keys to Lincoln-Douglas* by Travis Herche (2013)

Keeping Score

Once you get into competition, you'll discover the thrill of keeping up with your fellow competitors. My coaches and I, too, like to keep tabs on student performance and success. It's all part of the fun of the speech and debate community, as you'll soon find out. There are several ways to "keep score" and stay plugged in.

The **National Christian Homeschool Speech & Debate Rankings** is an inclusive ranking system for all homeschool competitors: *www.speechranks.com*. The site is underwritten and owned by Stoa, but may include any homeschool competitor who opens a profile. Scores from tournaments that have transparent tabulation rooms are able to upload results that are placed automatically into personal profiles. Otherwise, students are able to upload their own data manually.

There are two ways data is entered into *speechranks.com*. First, students may enter data themselves. If a student knows the number of people who competed in their event, and he knows the placing of how well he did, he may enter the data accordingly. If errors are discovered, a flagging system is managed to correct bad data. If a student does not know her placing, she at least receives one point but is assumed to have placed last.

The second way to enter data is for tournament directors to enter it with a spreadsheet. And Stoa works with TDs – both in and out of Stoa – to enter data with a simple upload. The process works quite smoothly, automatically correcting any student-entered errors. All Stoa tournaments and many non-qualifying NCFCA tournaments have open tabulation rooms, which are, as the name implies, tabulation rooms where results are open to observation by all competitors.

The way I see it, though, keeping track of student performance is fun – and beneficial. It heightens the sense of *sport* in speech and debate. And it can spur participants on to greater achievement. I have literally sat in front of *speechranks.com* and clicked for hours, just like a kid reading stats on baseball cards. And one of the most exciting things to realize is that colleges and employers may do the same! Indeed, the founders of the site hope that students can point online to their competitive results, and those results can lead to scholarships, job offers and other opportunities.

An online database for scoring is one thing, but I've found the world of social media to actually network students. It has been incredible to see the world become very, very small as students who live on the other side of the country connect in a personal way through Facebook.

Training Minds has a Facebook page! We'd love for you to become a fan and keep in touch with the events and discussion: *www.facebook.com/trainingminds.*

Commitment

Training Minds – though a small organization with a specific focus – has a huge impact in people's lives. Our camps, coaching and curriculum create a lot of tremendous stories in young people's lives, and I'd like to share with you one story, one that involves three students threaded together over the past several years. They're ready for action:

- **Cody Herche.** I've mentioned Cody earlier. He's a debate legend, 2006 Titlist, and author of *Keys to Cross-Examination*. He hasn't been a Training Minds coach for the past couple years because he is pursuing a law degree at Cornell. Last summer he had an internship that only the top students in his class earned. He gave me this complement: "Without Training Minds coaching in my portfolio, I would have never made it this far." I'm bubbling proud of Cody.

- **Shane Baumgardner.** When Cody was coaching, he spent a good deal of time on Shane, a young man with a solid head on his shoulders. Cody mentored and trained him. Shane, together with his debate partner Kaitlin, became even bigger legends in debate. At one point, they won 40 ballots in a row without losing a single one. Both of them became Training Minds coaches after high school graduation. Shane is currently studying law at the University of Minnesota at the very young age of 18. He returned to Colorado late last year to marry his former debate partner, Kaitlin, and they're now in Minnesota to finish the law degree.

- **Brooke Wade.** Shane's student was a young lady in Florida. She is just as optimistic as Shane was, and Shane coached her at our Florida camp and beyond. Just like Shane bested Cody's performance in extemp, Brooke followed suit. She took the last two year's NCFCA Titles in Extemp. Brooke is now Training Minds' youngest coach.

This is just a taste of the tremendous heritage we're building at Training Minds. I have many stories that are just as encouraging. I wanted to share this with you because I honestly believe Training Minds is the best investment you can make in young people.

Sure, I'm biased. I love these kids and I want nothing but the best for their future. But you know what? Training Minds played a big part in their growing up, and I want to give the same to other kids in the future.

Of course, this takes financial support. If you want to help give to the most exciting future of kids like Cody, Shane and Brooke, check out *www.trainingminds.org/donate*.

Who wouldn't want to be part of this community?

CHAPTER 7

Conclusion

Last summer I led the largest forensics tournament in recent history, the largest *ever* in the 16 years of homeschool speech and debate. Six hundred forensics competitors gathered in Colorado Springs for Stoa's National Invitational Tournament of Champions. We had nearly 2,500 people at the awards ceremony, the last awards to be given out for the year. Hundreds of trophies were awarded, and of the dozen title trophies, my son and another one of my students took titles home. I was so bubbling proud. It felt like the pinnacle of my career.

A few short months later we were at it again, except it was the beginning of the new year. We hosted a tournament on the basement floor of a church. Instead of 600 students we had 80, one-third of them brand new at this speech and debate "thing," many of the parents not knowing what was going on. It was a 1-day debate qualifier that clunked along. We ended the day just as proud, very much like a few months before when it seemed we had the entire nation in our presence.

It doesn't really matter whether you become a champ or not, or whether you host the largest tournament ever or not. What matters is that you are *actively participating in life*. If there is anything I'd like you to take away from this activity of speech and debate, it is that you would *act* upon the skills you learn to contribute to the world in a positive way.

I serve as president of Training Minds, the 501c3 nonprofit organization that spends its time and energy opening up opportunities for students to compete. We take the mandate to train our minds seriously, especially the minds of children. As stated on its website:

> **The goal of Training Minds is to provide "training grounds" for youth to effectively train their minds for action, particularly in the areas of debate, speech, logic and reasoning, to grow into confident individuals who see value in engaging the culture for common good.**

Do you agree with this goal? It is to train your mind for action. I believe it is for big and awesome things.

And do you get the idea of the training going on? We are building up a generation of great communicators through speech and debate. It is truly awesome to see what they will become, what they will do for the good of the world we launch them in.

See you at some tournaments, my friend!

Acknowledgements

There are a ton of fantastic people in the speech and debate community, it is impossible to thank them all. I may be bubbling with enthusiasm, but it is because of so many people who have brought out the best in me. Specifically...

My Training Minds Coaches: Matthew Erickson, Matthew Baker, Cody Herche, Chase Harrington, Mark Mittelberg, Matthew Mittelberg, Rob Parks, Maggie Carabelos, Brooke Wade, Luis Garcia, Travis Herche, Cynthia Jeub, Jon Bateman, Mike Winther, Larry Sparks, Jesse Byrnes, Derek Martin, Shane Baumgardner, and Kaitlin (formerly Nelson) Baumgardner.

I must recognize two coaches from the rest. First, Vance Trefethen, who has been with me the longest, and he has been a wonderful friend and business partner. Second, my friend Kim Anderson, who passed away last summer after a good fight with cancer. Kim, you impacted countless lives through your good work here, and you will be missed.

Many educators of communication have influenced me over the years. Many thanks to Prof./Asst. Profs: Leland, Myers, Littlefield, Rutledge, Bennett and Hack. Keep teaching those of us who share in your enthusiasm.

My modest-sized club, Monumentum, your enthusiasm is contagious. Let's keep winning tournaments!

My kids are awesome, this year with five at competitor-age. I sure love you guys. We have many joyous years ahead of us.

And my dearest Wendy. You know you pull the best out of me, always encouraging and most of all loving.

Connect with Chris Jeub

I have a blog, and I'd like you to connect with me by subscribing.

I must disclose, though, that I blog about other things than just speech and debate. I like to post quotes from books I'm reading, brag about my crazy-large family, discuss philosophy and entrepreneurism and education, sometimes even geek out over the latest technology. It's a blog, mind you, and the posts reflect my life, my thoughts, and my passions.

You know what? That's very similar to what I'm trying to get across in *Jeub's Guide to Speech & Debate*. There is an incredible life ahead of you that I want you to speak up about. You're in training to fight (or debate) the dragons out there that try to intellectually stomp down your ambitions. I want you to live fully alive, without apology, and do the great things you were created to do.

You can start by joining me on my journey. Subscribe to my blog and join in the conversations that roll in the community of speakers and debaters living life to the fullest. There's probably a free download when you do, but you're in it for more than that. You and I are going to become friends and take on this thing called life.

Subscribe at
www.chrisjeub.com/connect